VAN GOGH
MUSEUM

VINCENT VAN GOGH

LIFE, WORK
AND CONTEMPORARIES

A MUSEUM FOR VAN GOGH

The Van Gogh Museum in Amsterdam attracts more than 1 million visitors every year from all over the world. It is hard to imagine that lack of interest in Vincent van Gogh's art during his lifetime drove the artist to the brink of despair. The mythical stature that Van Gogh has subsequently acquired in the eyes of so many people, the reverence in which his work is held and the millions who have read his letters, all contrast dramatically with Van Gogh's life and expectations.

His career as an artist lasted ten years, a relatively short period during which he produced some 1100 drawings and almost 900 paintings. By far the most important and diverse group of Van Gogh's works is to be found in the Van Gogh Museum. The core of the museum's collection is formed by the works owned by the Vincent van Gogh Foundation, comprising all the pieces formerly in the artist's family collection. This core collection consists of 200 paintings, almost 500 drawings, four sketchbooks and some 800 letters written by Vincent van Gogh, plus the private art collection assembled by Vincent and his brother Theo, comprising 570 Japanese prints, 1500 journal illustrations and works by artist friends, such as Henri de Toulouse-Lautrec, Paul Gauguin and Georges Seurat. Since the Van Gogh Museum first opened its doors Vincent and Theo's collection, which the brothers accumulated by purchasing or exchanging works, has served as a starting point for the museum's own collecting policy which focuses on expanding its collection through the acquisition of 19th-century art connected with Van Gogh and his period.

Over the past decades an ambition programme of collecting and exhibiting has made the Van Gogh Museum what it is today: a treasury of Van Gogh's finest works and a leading centre for Van Gogh-related expertise, where correspondence and family documents are stored and studied, presented and explained from constantly new perspectives. It is also a museum of the 19th century, with a varied and engaging programme of exhibitions about the period in which Van Gogh lived, and the art associated with him.

This book guides the reader through the life and work of Van Gogh, making constant connections with important pieces by other artists from the period 1830 to 1914, which the museum has used to expand its collection over past decades. This approach reflects the Van Gogh Museum's stated ambition, to create an art-historical background against which Van Gogh's work may be better understood, and thereby presenting his unique position as a 19th-century artist within an international context.

John Leighton Director

Well – my plan for my life is to produce paintings
and drawings, as many as I can and the best that I can;
then, when my life is over all I hope is that I shall
depart it looking back with love and nostalgia, and thinking:
oh, the paintings I might have made!
– Vincent van Gogh, 11 November 1883

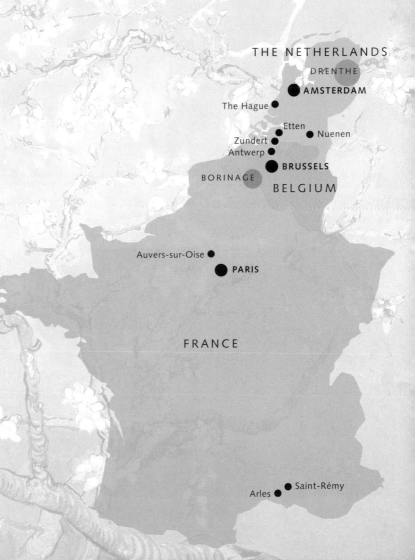

Zundert	* 30.03.1853
The Borinage	1878–1880
Brussels	1880–1881
Etten	1881
The Hague	1881–1883
Drenthe	1883
Nuenen	1883–1885
Antwerp	1885–1886
Paris	1886–1888
Arles	1888–1889
Saint-Rémy	1889–1890
Auvers-sur-Oise	1890
Auvers-sur-Oise	† 29.07.1890

THE NETHERLANDS

DRENTHE

AMSTERDAM

The Hague

Etten

Nuenen

Zundert

Antwerp

BRUSSELS

BORINAGE

BELGIUM

Auvers-sur-Oise

PARIS

FRANCE

Arles Saint-Rémy

THE EARLY YEARS

Vincent van Gogh was born on 30 March 1853 in Zundert in Brabant, the son of protestant minister Theodorus van Gogh and his wife Anna Carbentus. The couple had a further five children, one of whom, Theo (1857-1891), would play a crucial role in Van Gogh's life. Little is known about Vincent's early years. Family members described him as an introverted, somewhat peculiar boy, who showed no sign that he would one day emerge as a major talent.

When Van Gogh was 16 years old, he found a position in The Hague as junior assistant at the French firm of art dealers Goupil & Cie. Here the foundations were laid for his interest in visual art.

Van Gogh had a flair for the business and was transferred to the firm's London branch in 1873 in order to gain more experience.

Vincent van Gogh at the age of 19

Art dealers Goupil & Cie in The Hague

Working for a firm of art dealers brought Van Gogh into contact with artists of the Barbizon School, such as Charles-François Daubigny. He was highly impressed by this French painter whose landscapes were simple and unpretentious. Other Barbizon School artists who appealed to Van Gogh were Jean-François Millet, Camille Corot and Théodore Rousseau.

Charles-François Daubigny *October,* date unknown, oil on canvas (on loan from the Rijksmuseum, Amsterdam, gift of Baroness M.C. van Lynden-van Pallandt)

Preacher

In 1875 Van Gogh was transferred again, to Goupil's Paris headquarters. From this moment onwards his letters to his family show increasing evidence of an intense preoccupation with religion; he now wanted to help the weaker members of society, an ambition that would be difficult to fulfil as an art dealer. After Van Gogh was dismissed from his job at Goupil's, in 1876, he decided to become a protestant minister but soon abandoned the preparatory studies for such a career. Despite this setback Van Gogh immediately found a position as a lay preacher in the Belgian mining district, the Borinage. Although his involvement with the impoverished inhabitants earned him the nickname 'Christ of the Coal Mine', it was also the reason why his appointment as a preacher was not extended.

An awakening artist

After this failure Van Gogh suffered a crisis. He was 27 years old and no longer knew what to do with his life. His entire family came up with ideas for a possible career, and Theo finally suggested that Vincent might train as an artist. Initially Van Gogh was less than enthusiastic. Although he had regularly drawn for pleasure since childhood, becoming a professional artist was another matter, and he was not sure he would be able to master technicalities such as perspective. Eventually, however, Van Gogh's need to give artistic expression to his ideas about the essence of life gained the upper hand, though he would continue to have mixed feelings about his career as an artist throughout his life. A major reason for these doubts was his constant need to receive financial support from Theo. The brothers agreed that Vincent would regularly send drawings and paintings to Theo, in return for this support.

Self-tuition and painting lessons

In order to master his chosen profession Van Gogh spent some time in Brussels. He pored over textbooks on anatomy and perspective, and taught himself as he worked, studying intensely pieces by contemporaries and old masters. When life in the city proved too expensive, Van Gogh decided to stay with his parents in Etten. Here he looked for models to draw amongst the peasant population.

In early 1880, when Van Gogh had just decided to become an artist, he went on
a walking tour from the Borinage in Belgium to Courrières in France, a round trip
of 120 kilometres. Courrières was the home of the artist-poet Jules Breton,
whom Van Gogh admired as a 'peasant painter'. However, he was too shy to
visit Breton's studio and turned for home without achieving his aim. This painting
by Breton shows the church tower of Courrières in the distance.

Jules Breton *Young peasant girl with a hoe,* 1882, oil on canvas

Following a quarrel with his father Van Gogh moved to The Hague at the end of 1881. He had pinned his hopes on a cousin by marriage, the painter Anton Mauve, from whom he wanted to learn the rudiments of drawing, painting and work in watercolour. During his initial months in The Hague Van Gogh drew many figure studies and city views. From the summer of 1882 he began to experiment with oils.

This drawing is one of Van Gogh's earliest copies after Millet's
The sower. During his life he produced more than 30 drawings
and paintings on this theme.

Vincent van Gogh *The sower (after Millet)*, 1881, pencil, pen and brush in ink and watercolour

Anton Mauve *Sheep on the heath near Laren*, c. 1887, transparent watercolour

In The Hague Van Gogh mainly concentrated on drawing. He composed this scene of people waiting in front of the lottery office from various sketches drawn on location.

Vincent van Gogh *The poor and money,* 1882, chalk, watercolour and ink on paper

During his time in The Hague, in 1883, Van Gogh became acquainted with the work of Léon Augustin Lhermitte, which he had previously only known from black-and-white reproductions. 'It seems to me that Lhermitte's secret can only be that he knows the figure in general, and the sturdy, stern figure of the working man in particular, through and through, and plucks his motifs from the heart of the people.' Van Gogh probably saw this large canvas of a group of haymakers later in his career, at Goupil's art gallery in Paris.

Léon Augustin Lhermitte *Haymaking,* 1887, oil on canvas

enen schets

maar en de aquarel zelf is geen zwart dan in 't

ar op dat schetsje het zwart 't donkerst is zullen

achten en de aquarel. — donker groen

aauw. Nu adieu, en geloof me dat z

en hartelijk om lach dat de lui mij zi

ts anders ben dan een vriend van de nat

de van werk — ook van menschen voor

'I am so glad that we have so much in common, not only memories of times past, but that you are working in the same business where I was until recently and so know many people and places that I know too, and have so much love for nature and art.'
– letter to Theo, 28 April 1876

Van Gogh's surviving correspondence comprises more than 900 letters. The earliest of these dates from 29 September 1872, and is addressed to his brother Theo, to whom Van Gogh wrote the majority of his letters. The final letter dates from July 1890, and was written in the week of the artist's death. Thanks to this correspondence it is possible to follow Van Gogh's life from close at hand. In an age before the telephone became widely used, writing letters was the only way to maintain long-distance contact with friends and family. Van Gogh used the medium of pen and paper to discuss the problems he was tackling, in both his work and private life, his extensive musings on art, literature and religion, and also everyday occurrences.

Van Gogh's letters contain a wealth of information about his sources of inspiration, his methods and his thoughts. He was an impassioned writer, so his letters are fascinating, even literary, documents. His wide-ranging descriptions of the things he saw and the locations where he worked betray his artist's eye. Van Gogh regularly included sketches in his letters, in order to illustrate the drawings and paintings he was working on. In the Van Gogh Museum there are some 730 of the artist's letters, which he wrote to his brother Theo, other family members and friends. Researchers are currently working in the museum on the first scholarly edition of Van Gogh's correspondence.

Theo van Gogh in 1889

VAN GOGH'S LETTERS

VINCENT VAN GOGH

< **Vincent van Gogh** *Letter sketch in letter to Theo*, 31 July 1882

DRENTHE, NUENEN AND ANTWERP

In 1883, fired by the enthusiastic stories of his artist friend Anthon van Rappard, Van Gogh went to the northern province of Drenthe where he intended to paint the peasants' authentic way of life. But lack of money and models soon made the attractions of the picturesque landscape and its hardworking inhabitants fade. The peat workers refused to accept the eccentric artist. Lonely and disillusioned Van Gogh left Drenthe after only three months and moved back in with his parents who were now living in the parsonage at Nuenen.

Here Van Gogh renewed his search for distinctive models. He worked obsessively on portrait studies of peasants and artisans and painted his famous work *The potato eaters*. Not long after this painting was completed, however, the pastor forbade the villagers to pose for Van Gogh any longer. In November 1885 he moved to Antwerp, thinking that he might be able to earn some money as an artist there. He enrolled at the Antwerp art academy in order to improve his drawing skills.

Vincent van Gogh *Cottages in Drenthe*, 1883, oil on canvas

Vincent van Gogh *The parsonage at Nuenen,* 1885, oil on canvas

Vincent van Gogh *Weaver*, 1884, pencil, ink and watercolour

Vincent van Gogh *The kingfisher,* 1884, charcoal on paper

If a peasant painting smells of bacon, smoke and potato steam, fine – that's not unhealthy – if a stable smells of manure – alright, that's what you get with a stable (...). But a peasant painting should not be perfumed.
– letter to Theo, April 1885

The potato eaters

During the winter of 1885 Van Gogh was in Nuenen where he produced a considerable number of studies of peasant heads in oil. He intended to follow these with a large painting of figures in a single composition that Theo might be able to exhibit in Paris. The De Groot family of Nuenen posed for the figure painting. 'This week I plan to start on that thing with peasants around a dish of potatoes in the evening, or perhaps I shall make daylight of it, or both – or neither you'll say.' Van Gogh eventually opted for the difficult task of depicting the potato eaters by the light of an oil lamp, which allowed him to practice 'painting dark that is nevertheless colour'.

To Theo he wrote: 'I wanted the canvas to convey a completely different way of life than ours, than that of civilised people. So I should definitely not want everyone simply to consider it handsome or good.' The work unleashed a great deal of criticism, although Theo reported from Paris that some artists thought it 'promising'. At the time it was inconceivable that *The potato eaters* would one day become one of Van Gogh's most famous paintings.

Vincent van Gogh *Three hands, two with a fork*, 1885, chalk on paper

THE POTATO EATERS

VINCENT VAN GOGH

< **Vincent van Gogh** *The potato eaters* (detail), 1885, oil on canvas

Vincent van Gogh *The potato eaters,* 1885, oil on canvas

Jozef Israëls enjoyed international success with his painting *A frugal meal* from 1878, in which the central motif was a simple peasant meal. The artist would subsequently produce many more scenes depicting this subject, such as *A peasant family at the table* from 1882, which it is thought Van Gogh saw during his time in The Hague.

Jozef Israëls *A peasant family at the table,* 1882, oil on canvas

At the end of 1885 Van Gogh wrote to Theo that he wanted to come to Paris. Theo was working there as an art dealer at the firm of Boussod, Valadon & Cie (formerly Goupil's). Van Gogh was increasingly bothered by the fact that his brother was supporting him financially. He wanted to stand on his own feet and intended to become a pupil of the then well-known painter Fernand Cormon, whose studio was located on Boulevard de Clichy. Theo wrote back that he would not be able to accommodate his brother immediately, owing to lack of space. But Van Gogh was determined to pursue his career as an artist and turned up in Paris without warning around 1 March 1886. He moved into Theo's tiny apartment in the artists' neighbourhood of Montmartre, which the brothers would later leave, for a larger apartment in Rue Lepic.

Vincent van Gogh *Vegetable gardens and the Moulin Blute-Fin on Montmartre*, 1887, oil on canvas

Vincent van Gogh *View of Paris from Vincent's room in the Rue Lepic*, 1887, oil on canvas

Artistic contacts

In Paris a whole new world opened up for Van Gogh. He became acquainted with the work of Jean-François Millet and Eugène Delacroix, which he had previously only known from books, and saw paintings by impressionists such as Édouard Manet and Claude Monet for the first time. He met Henri de Toulouse-Lautrec, who specialised in depicting Parisian café life, and followed Lautrec's example in his painting of Agostina Segatori. Van Gogh also came into contact with Paul Signac and his 'dot method', later dubbed pointillism, a painting technique based on splitting light into its separate colour components. From 1886 Van Gogh spent time with the young artist Émile Bernard whose dark-contoured, decorative 'Japanese' style he would later imitate. Theo's work as an art dealer also furnished Van Gogh with many artistic contacts. In November 1887, for example, he met Paul Gauguin who had just returned from a trip to Martinique. A year later the two artists would work together briefly but intensively in Arles in southern France, a collaboration that would change Van Gogh's life and work.

From dark to light

Paris inspired Van Gogh to paint city views, still lives and self-portraits. In the summer of 1886 he painted many flower still lives, inspired by such sources as the work of Adolphe Monticelli. These studies served as colour experiments in the artist's search for a more distinctive palette. Van Gogh also produced 27 self-portraits in Paris. Although he was unable to pay for models, he was determined to master the art of portraiture as he thought this might earn him some money in the future, and it cost him nothing to paint himself. These self-portraits reflect the change in Van Gogh's painting style - from a dark to a light palette - which largely occurred during his Paris period.

Exchanging and collecting art

Theo and Vincent's art collection was growing steadily. Vincent regularly exchanged his own work for pieces by artist friends, and Theo occasionally bought work from contemporaries. The collection thus assembled by the Van Gogh brothers is currently housed in the Van Gogh Museum.

Vincent van Gogh *Still life with quinces and lemons*, 1887, oil on canvas

This is a portrait of Agostina Segatori, owner of the Café du Tambourin, with whom Van Gogh had an affair lasting several months in 1887. In Agostina's café the artist organised an exhibition of his own collection of Japanese prints.

Vincent van Gogh *Agostina Segatori in the Café du Tambourin*, 1887, oil on canvas

Henri de Toulouse-Lautrec *Poudre de riz*, 1887, oil on canvas

Adolphe Monticelli *Flower still life,* 1875, oil on canvas

Vincent van Gogh *Vase with gladioli and Chinese asters*, 1886, oil on canvas

You see, we love Japanese painting, we are subject to its influence [...] all impressionists have this in common [...].
– letter to Theo, 5 June 1888

Vincent van Gogh *The courtesan (after Eisen),* 1887, oil on canvas

Japanese influences

In Antwerp Van Gogh had pinned a number of Japanese woodcuts on the wall. 'You know, those little female figures in gardens or on the beach, horsemen, flowers, gnarled and thorny branches.' He was attracted by the clarity of the prints, the brilliant colours and amusing details. Van Gogh was not alone in appreciating the daring compositions and cropped images of Japanese woodcuts. After Japan had opened up to the outside world around 1870, many western artists had come into contact with these prints, which were imported in great numbers. Established impressionists such as Manet and Monet made use of Japanese elements in their work, while younger artists such as Van Gogh's friend Émile Bernard also discovered this eastern source of inspiration. In Paris Van Gogh began to collect decorative Japanese prints; he also painted three copies in oil after these. His decision to travel to southern France was associated with his hope that he would find light and colour there, plus subjects in a 'Japanese' mood. 'The emotion which the route from Paris to Arles produced in me is still fresh in my memory. How I looked to see if it was already Japanese yet! Childish, don't you think?' Van Gogh found his subjects in 'Japanese' mood in the blossoming trees, sun-drenched summer landscapes and colourful inhabitants of Provence.

JAPANESE INFLUENCES

VINCENT VAN GOGH

< **Vincent van Gogh** *The flowering plum tree (after Hiroshige)* (detail), 1887, oil on canvas

Utagawa Hiroshige *The Plum tree teahouse at Kameido*, 1857, woodcut

Vincent van Gogh *The flowering plum tree (after Hiroshige),* 1887, oil on canvas

Utagawa Hiroshige *Sudden shower on the Great Bridge near Atake*, 1857, woodcut

Vincent van Gogh *The bridge in the rain (after Hiroshige)*, 1887, oil on canvas

In 1888 Van Gogh decided to go in search of colourful landscapes, moving from Paris to the small town of Arles in Provence. His health had deteriorated somewhat and he hoped that the warmth of the south would help him to recover from the effects of city life. Van Gogh's expectations were not disappointed. He arrived in Arles in the spring, and though there was still snow on the ground the almond trees were already in blossom. Shortly after his arrival Van Gogh devoted himself to painting orchards full of blossoming fruit trees. He intended to hang these works together, to create a 'decoration' that represented the season of spring.

Vincent van Gogh *Letter sketch in letter to Theo*, 13 April 1888

VINCENT VAN GOGH

Vincent van Gogh *The pink orchard*, 1888, oil on canvas

Vincent van Gogh *The pink peach tree,* 1888, oil on canvas

VINCENT VAN GOGH

Vincent van Gogh *The white orchard,* 1888, oil on canvas

Vincent van Gogh *Rock with trees: Montmajour*, 1888, pencil and East Indian ink

VINCENT VAN GOGH

Vincent van Gogh *The harvest*, 1888, oil on canvas

Once Gauguin had been persuaded to come to Arles, an artistic dialogue developed between the two artists. The little town and its inhabitants provided the inspiration for an impressive series of landscapes and portraits. Although Van Gogh and Gauguin's collaboration initially led to new experiments in painting technique, their moody temperaments quickly disrupted the relationship. Irritation grew on both sides and erupted in violent arguments shortly before Christmas 1888. Van Gogh began to display the first signs of his illness. During an attack in which he became totally disoriented Van Gogh cut off a piece of his left ear. Two days later Gauguin departed Arles for good and Van Gogh was admitted to hospital. His high hopes for a Studio of the South had come to nothing.

In Arles Van Gogh made new friends, such as Roulin the postman and his family, all of whom posed for the artist. Roulin's wife Augustine brought her baby Marcelle with her and Vincent made several oil studies

Vincent van Gogh *Portrait of Marcelle Roulin*, 1888, oil on canvas

Van Gogh 'portrayed' Paul Gauguin in a still life of the only elaborate chair in the 'Yellow House'. He chose a wooden kitchen chair for his own 'self-portrait', a painting now in the National Gallery in London. Van Gogh used the contrast between his own ordinary chair and Gauguin's elegant seat to represent his admiration for Gauguin as an artist and a person.

Vincent van Gogh *Gauguin's chair*, 1888, oil on canvas

I am painting with the enthusiasm of a Marseillais eating bouillabaisse, something that will not surprise you when what I am painting are large sunflowers.

– letter to Theo, 21 or 22 August 1888

Vincent van Gogh *Sunflowers run to seed*, 1887, oil on canvas

Sunflowers

Van Gogh first painted sunflowers in Paris, in the summer of 1887, and returned to the theme in Arles a year later. Here, he planned to produce a series of sunflower painting against various blue backgrounds, to decorate the studio in the Yellow House. Van Gogh painted three of these works with a blue background and one version of the sunflower theme with a yellow background. Although he did not complete his decorative series, he hung two sunflower canvases, including the largely yellow work, in the bedroom where Gauguin came to stay. After Gauguin had left Arles, he wrote to Van Gogh asking for the two sunflower paintings from his former room. Van Gogh was unwilling to part with these so he painted a copy of both works. The version of the theme with the yellow background, the famous still life entitled *Sunflowers*, is one of the highlights of the Van Gogh Museum collection.

< **Vincent van Gogh** *Sunflowers* (detail), 1889, oil on canvas

Paul Gauguin *Van Gogh painting sunflowers*, 1888, oil on jute

Vincent van Gogh *Sunflowers*, 1889, oil on canvas

Van Gogh's life and work were considerably influenced by mental and physical ailments. All his experiences were intense, he was extremely emotional and he poured his heart and soul into everything. His parents had started to worry about their 'neurotic' son from an early age and had little faith that he would make a success of his life. Once Van Gogh had decided to become an artist, Theo kept an eye on his older brother from a distance. But even he could not prevent Vincent from regularly neglecting himself, as a result of excessive work and lack of money. During these periods Van Gogh would live for days on bread and coffee. In Paris he also drank too much alcohol. This lifestyle caused him all kinds of physical afflictions, including bad teeth and stomach problems. In southern France Van Gogh suffered his first delusional 'attacks' 'If it were mine to wish I would ask [God], take him to You, but we have to take what God gives us', his mother sighed after Van Gogh had cut off part of his ear in 1888. Van Gogh's illness has provoked a great deal of speculation. It is conjectured that he suffered from a form of epilepsy, whose symptoms worsened during periods of physical neglect. The artist's nervous character did nothing to improve the situation, and he experienced fits of depression and despair.

Claude-Émile Schuffenecker *Copy of Van Gogh's self-portrait*, undated, chalk on paper

VAN GOGH'S ILLNESS

VINCENT VAN GOGH

< **Vincent van Gogh** *Courtyard of the hospital at Arles* (detail), 1889, ink on paper

Vincent van Gogh *Irises,* 1890, oil on canvas

This painting was inspired by the birth of Van Gogh's nephew Vincent Willem, the son of his brother Theo and sister-in-law Jo. Van Gogh painted the almond blossom in a decorative composition with a Japanese flavour. When the canvas was finished he sent the work to the new parents as a gift. Jo later wrote that the baby was fascinated by the sky-blue painting that hung in their bedroom.

Vincent van Gogh *Almond blossom*, 1890, oil on canvas

Christy alone has been the only one of the philosophers, magi etc to have stamped eternal life, the infinity of time, the nullity of death, the necessity and sense of serenity and dedication, as the most important certainty. He lived serenely, as an artist greater than all other artists (...)

– letter to Émile Bernard, 23 June 1888

Vincent van Gogh *Still life with Bible*, 1885, oil on canvas

Religion

The son of a protestant minister, Van Gogh was brought up in a protestant environment. However, he gradually distanced himself from official forms of Christianity and discovered a more personal kind of religion, centred on the gospel. He struggled with his desire to be useful, and came to the conclusion that he could also serve God as an artist. 'Try to understand the essence of what the great artists, the serious masters, are saying in their masterpieces, you will recognise God in this. One has written or said it in a book, the other in a painting,' he thought. Van Gogh also called Christ an 'artist, greater than all other artists, disdaining marble, clay and paint, working in living flesh'.

Van Gogh could be deeply moved by religious scenes, and various artistic motifs with biblical associations, such as the sower, the harvest and the olive tree, can be found in his work. However, he rarely depicted biblical subjects, as he found it difficult to represent religious motifs in a respectful manner without creating something that seemed to him crude and coarse. For this reason Van Gogh only produced 'translations in colour' of works by other artists whom he believed had managed to depict Christian themes in an appropriate fashion.

RELIGION

VINCENT VAN GOGH

< **Vincent van Gogh** *The sower* (detail), 1888, oil on canvas

'The figure of Christ has only been painted by Delacroix and Rembrandt in the way that I perceive him', Van Gogh declared. This is a copy after a lithograph of Delacroix's *Pietà*, with Christ's face a self-portrait of Van Gogh.

Vincent van Gogh *Pietà (after Eugène Delacroix)*, 1889, oil on canvas

Vincent van Gogh *The raising of Lazarus (after Rembrandt),* 1890, oil on canvas

Vincent van Gogh *The sower,* 1888, oil on canvas

'In the reaper', Van Gogh wrote to Theo, 'I saw the image of death, in the sense that the corn being cut down represents mankind. If you like it is thus the antithesis of the sower that I previously attempted.'

Vincent van Gogh *Wheatfield with a reaper,* 1889, oil on canvas

In May 1890 Van Gogh left the asylum and travelled back to the north. On the advice of Theo and Camille Pissarro he took up residence in the artists' village of Auvers-sur-Oise, close to Paris, under the supervision of a local doctor, Paul-Ferdinand Gachet. The beautiful countryside initially proved beneficial to the artist. During the last two months of his life he abandoned himself to drawing and painting, producing almost a work a day. In early June, however, Theo wrote to his brother that he was tired of working for Boussod and was considering starting his own business; he warned Vincent that they would both have to tighten their belts. Van Gogh was deeply affected by Theo's dissatisfaction: 'My life too has been assailed at its root, I too no longer stand firm on my feet.'

Vincent van Gogh *Old vineyard with peasant woman*, 1890, pencil and watercolour

VINCENT VAN GOGH

Vincent van Gogh *View of Auvers*, 1890, oil on canvas

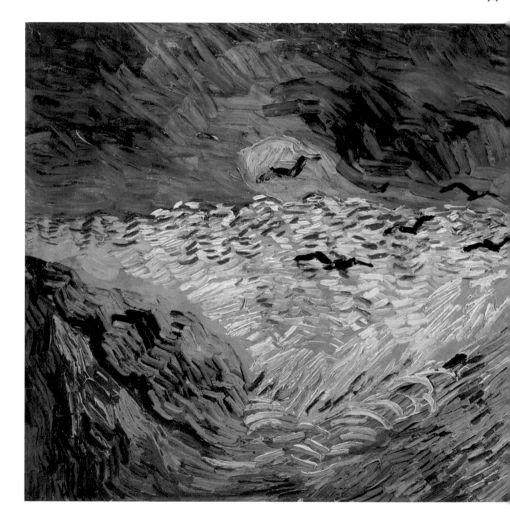

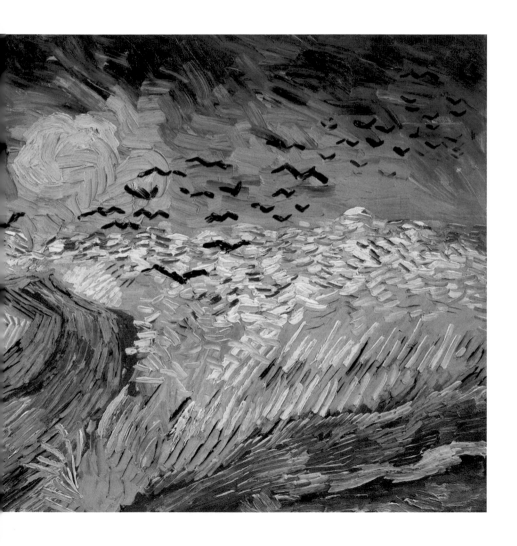

Vincent van Gogh *Wheatfield with crows,* 1890, oil on canvas

The Van Gogh family collection

After the death of his brother Theo van Gogh found himself in possession of a large art collection, containing all the drawings and paintings that Vincent had sent him over the years in exchange for financial support, plus his own collection of works by artist friends and neo-impressionists. He was determined to establish Vincent's reputation. But a few months later Theo himself became seriously ill and died in January 1891, barely six months after his brother's death.

His young widow, Jo van Gogh-Bonger, shared Theo's ambitions, for she was convinced of the importance of Van Gogh's art, and she administered the Van Gogh collection on behalf of her young son Vincent Willem with drive and passion. She organised exhibitions to gain publicity for the works, sold paintings to art dealers and prepared the first Dutch edition of Vincent and Theo's correspondence. This was published in 1914, the year in which Jo also had Theo reburied in Auvers, beside his brother.

Jo van Gogh-Bonger, at home with her son and second husband, c. 1905. On the wall are two works by Van Gogh, *The bridge of Langlois* and *The harvest*.

< Vincent and Theo's grave (photo Ed van der Elsken, 1952)

During the early years of the 20th century international interest in Van Gogh's work grew rapidly. One of the most enthusiastic Van Gogh collectors was Helene Kröller-Müller. By the 1930s she already owned around 80 paintings and 200 drawings by the artist. These works are now in the Kröller-Müller Museum in Otterlo.

A new museum

When Jo van Gogh-Bonger died in 1925, her son Vincent Willem took over administration of the family art collection. Although these works could be seen in the Stedelijk Museum in Amsterdam from 1930 onwards, they did not have any permanent accommodation. In 1962 the newly established Vincent van Gogh Foundation acquired the collection with financial support from the Dutch government. The Foundation placed the collection on permanent loan to the Dutch state which commissioned construction of the Van Gogh Museum. The building, designed by the renowned architect Gerrit Rietveld, opened its doors in 1973. Paintings from the Van Gogh family collection still form the core of the museum's permanent collection. Although Van Gogh's drawings

The Van Gogh Museum

are rarely exhibited on account of their fragility, selections of drawings and prints can regularly be seen in both print cabinets in the museum.

Increasing public interest and the museum's determination to organise exhibitions on 19th-century art as well as Van Gogh's works led to the opening of a new exhibition wing in 1999. Every year three to five exhibitions on art associated with Van Gogh and his age are organised in this striking, semi-circular wing, designed by the Japanese architect Kisho Kurokawa. These temporary exhibitions allow the permanent collection to be seen within a broader context and enable the Van Gogh Museum to present itself as 'a museum of the 19th century'.

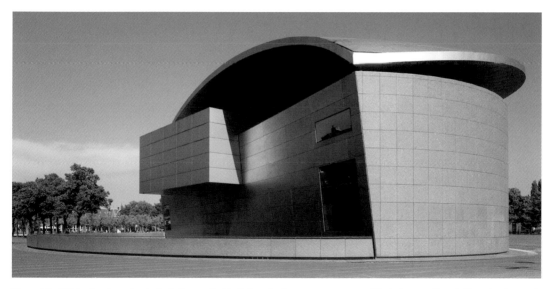

The architect Kisho Kurokawa is principally known for his designs for Japanese museums and Kuala Lumpur Airport. He makes frequent use of geometric forms and endeavours to achieve a marriage between eastern and western principles in philosophy and architecture.

The new exhibition wing at the Van Gogh Museum

The core of the collection is formed by works owned by the Vincent van Gogh Foundation. The museum also actively collects art from the period 1830-1914. In recent years the collection has been expanded and enriched with a number of major works. Impressionism, post-impressionism and neo-impressionism, realism and symbolism – all the movements are extremely well represented. The museum has also been presented with several valuable art collections. Since 1996 the Van Gogh Museum has managed the Bonger Collection, on loan from the Dutch state. This impressive collection of works, by artists such as Odilon Redon, Henri de Toulouse-Lautrec and Émile Bernard, once belonged to Andries Bonger, Theo van Gogh's friend and brother-in-law. In 2002, with the assistance of the Van Gogh Foundation, the museum also acquired a collection of more than 800 graphic works by the group of artists known as Les Nabis ('the prophets'), thereby bringing one of the most important collection of prints by these artists into the museum's possession.

Émile Bernard *Bernard's grandmother*, 1887, oil on canvas

VAN GOGH MUSEUM COLLECTION

VINCENT VAN GOGH

< **Georges Seurat** *The Seine at Courbevoie* (detail), 1884, oil on canvas

In this work Thomas Couture criticised the new movement in painting that chose to depict everyday subjects in preference to literary or historical themes. Van Gogh – a great admirer of the realists – painted motifs from his immediate environment, while Couture portrayed more lofty subjects in the academic tradition.

Thomas Couture *The realist*, 1865, oil on canvas

Van Gogh greatly admired work by the French realist Courbet. Like Courbet Van Gogh was scornful of academic painting with its high-minded narrative themes, and he described this style of art as 'stuffy' and 'tedious'.

Gustave Courbet *View of the Mediterranean at Maguelonne*, 1858, oil on canvas

Theo dealt in work by Claude Monet, and Van Gogh regularly hinted at his admiration for this painter. 'As for me, I shall work, and here and there something of my work will endure, but who shall be to the painted figure what Claude Monet is to landscape?' Monet painted these windmills during his first trip to the Netherlands, in 1871.

Claude Monet *Mills in the Westzijderveld near Zaandam,* 1871, oil on canvas

As a 'forerunner of impressionism' Édouard Manet helped to encourage the developments in painting that Van Gogh encountered in Paris. This harbour view draws its inspiration from Japanese prints, whose influence is evident in the horizontal composition, with its succession of layers, resembling stage scenery, and the 'cropping' of the scene.

Édouard Manet *The jetty of Boulogne-sur-Mer*, 1868, oil on canvas

Like Van Gogh and Paul Signac, Georges Seurat produced many small studies in the suburbs of Paris, working in a loose, impressionist style. These often served as a starting point for large canvases in a pointillist technique, in which he executed the scene in small dots painted with an almost mechanical regularity.

Georges Seurat *The Seine at Courbevoie*, 1884, oil on canvas

'I have read that an exhibition of the impressionists is coming at Durand-Ruel's. There will also be Caillebottes on display. I've seen nothing by him yet and I would like you to write and tell me what they're like.' (letter to Theo, May 1888)

Gustave Caillebotte *View from a balcony,* 1880, oil on canvas

Gauguin's *Leda and the swan* comes from the artist's Volpini series, a set of
11 zincographs, purchased by the Vincent van Gogh Foundation in 2004.

Paul Gauguin *Leda and the swan*, 1889, zincograph

Influenced by Japanese prints Henri de Toulouse-Lautrec developed a style characterised by an emphasis on colour planes, contours and silhouettes. The artist's exceptional colour lithographs, published in small limited editions, helped to give prints a new, higher status in the art world.

Henri de Toulouse-Lautrec *Poster for 'Le Missionnaire' (The loge with the gilded mascaron)*, 1894, coloured lithograph

Odilon Redon *Vase with flowers*, c. 1905, oil on canvas

Kees van Dongen is considered one of the fauve group of artists (from the French word 'fauve' meaning wild), whose name derives from the harsh colours and primitive forms they employed in their work. The fauves' use of colour and rough, thickly applied brushstrokes place them in a tradition that began with Van Gogh.

Kees van Dongen *Portrait of Guus Preitinger, the artist's wife*, 1911, oil on canvas

Scholarly research

The Van Gogh Museum collection forms a constant source of material for study and research. Curators, restorers and researchers work closely together to preserve, study and display the treasures in the museum's collection. Museum publications reflect the current state of research and report the latest findings. All the museum's research projects, which are often conducted in collaboration with international scientific and academic institutions, reinforce the museum's reputation as a world-class centre of expertise in 19th-century studies in general, and the life and work of Vincent van Gogh in particular.

Education and public services

A range of activities for children and adults accompanies the permanent collection and temporary exhibitions, thereby enhancing accessibility through the use of modern media such as the audio-tour and personal computer. In the children's studio young visitors can produce their own creative work, inspired by the art in the museum.

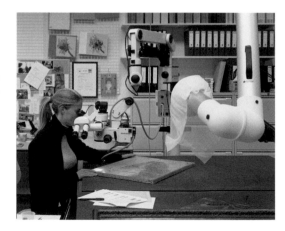

Scholarly research

Children's studio

Since 1990 the Van Gogh Museum has managed Museum Mesdag in The Hague. This museum, which retains a 19th-century style, is housed in the former home and studio of the artist H.W. Mesdag (1831-1915). Its fine collection of French and Dutch masters, including works by artists of the Barbizon and Hague School, effectively supplements the Van Gogh Museum's own collection. Museum Mesdag, 7f Laan van Meerdervoort, The Hague, is open from Tuesday to Sunday, from 12.00 to 17.00 hours.

Library and documentation

The Van Gogh Museum library, which is housed at 4 Muscumplein, forms a valuable source of information on the life and work of Vincent van Gogh and visual art from the period 1800-1920. The automated catalogue can be consulted online, via the museum website. The same building also accommodates the documentation department, which collects, manages and discloses documents associated with works in the Van Gogh Museum, including Van Gogh family correspondence.

VAN GOGH MUSEUM

VINCENT VAN GOGH

Room with cranes in Museum Mesdag, The Hague

Library and documentation

Editors John Leighton, Louis van Tilborgh, Chris Stolwijk, Caroline Breunesse, Heidi Vandamme, Suzanne Bogman, Josette van Gemert

Text Marie Baarspul

Translation Michèle Hendricks

Design Studio Roozen bv, Amsterdam

Printing bv Kunstdrukkerij Mercurius – Wormerveer

Photos Van Gogh Museum Luuk Kramer, 2005

Unless otherwise stated all the works reproduced belong to the Vincent van Gogh Foundation.

www.vangoghmuseumshop.com

Via www.vangoghmuseumshop.com articles can be sent from the Van Gogh Museum Shop all over the world. You can visit the site to order all Van Gogh Museum publications, stationery, accessories and reproductions of Van Gogh's paintings and drawings, almost 100 in total. Ordering online is safe and easy. All profits from the Van Gogh Museum Shop are reserved to finance the purchase of new works of art.

Van Gogh Museum

Paulus Potterstraat 7

1070 CX Amsterdam

The Netherlands

telephone +31 (0)20 570 52 00

fax +31 (0)20 570 52 22

e-mail info@vangoghmuseum.nl

website www.vangoghmuseum.nl

The Van Gogh Museum is open every day of the year, from 10 to 18 hours (except 1 January), and on Friday evenings until 22 hours.